Savannah

THEN AND NOW

In 1938, Major Bowes Advertising Company threw a parade as a salute to Savannah

Savannah

THEN AND NOW

created by:
Stefan Sanmann and John Crowell

new photography by:
Jeffrey Crowell

SAVANNAH HOUSE PUBLISHERS, INC.

Library of Congress Catalog Card Number:
97-61775

ISBN: 0-9654128-0-6

Published by:
Savannah House Publishers, Inc.
P.O. Box 14248
Savannah, GA 31401

Printed in Hong Kong

Acknowledgments

Savannah House Publishers would like to thank
the following for their gracious assistance in this book:

The Georgia Historical Society

Harry Haslam Sr.

Tommy Sheehan

Einar Throsdal III

Charley Spillane

Manfred Gebauer

Stephanie Nunn

Sam Humphries

And all the friendly people of
the Historic and Victorian Districts

Much remains of Savannah's rich heritage. Of the twenty four squares nestled between the Savannah River and Forsyth Park, only three have been lost. Thanks to efforts by organizations such as the Historic Savannah Foundation, a beautiful window to the past in danger of decay and demolition has been saved through restoration. Organizational and individual preservation projects which began appearing in the 1960's have dramatically increased through the 90's. The Historic and Victorian Districts have withstood withering assaults from natural disasters, misguided city councils and time itself.

Savannah, named after the surrounding grasslands, was founded on February 12, 1733 and incorporated into a city on December 23, 1789. The original plan laid out by James Oglethorpe consisted of four squares and accompanying wards. Development began slowly, and by 1851 Forsyth Park was laid out ending the Historic District at Gaston Street. Great fires broke out in 1796 and 1820, destroying many of the oldest structures near the river. The city was ravaged by yellow fever epidemics in 1820 and 1889. An earthquake shook downtown so hard in 1888, that many of the frame buildings had to be steadied with braces. Most of the houses and commercial buildings in the Historic and Victorian Districts were built during the prosperity brought by cotton exports during the 1800's. From the invention of the cotton gin in 1793 until the Union naval blockade of the Civil War, Savannah enjoyed wealth and growth. In 1864, Savannah was occupied by Union forces under General Sherman and was spared the complete destruction that befell Atlanta by a quick thinking mayor who surrendered the city. Until the 1890's, when cotton prices crashed, Savannah had become one of the South's great ports.

Beginning in the twenties, threats of a different nature appeared. Notions of progress caused a group of businessmen and civic leaders to attempt a very damaging modernization. Old buildings were razed or replaced with new boxlike structures. In 1935, the Montgomery Street squares were destroyed. There were plans to cut through the squares on Habersham Street in order to improve traffic flow. In the years between 1935 and 1955 many major historic landmarks were lost. Then in 1955, despite public resistance, the city destroyed the old City Market at Ellis Square, and leased the proerty to a parking garage. Later that year, the Historic Savannah Foundation was formed to save the Davenport House from demolition.

With the help of city bankers, the Historic Savannah Foundation purchased and resold endangered buildings to individuals who then restored them. Sadly, in 1962 the Union Station came down as part of an urban renewal project and was ultimately replaced by an entrance ramp to Interstate 16. Then, in 1966 the Historic Savannah Foundation took an inventory of the historic buildings downtown. A zoning ordinance that designated the downtown area a registered historical landmark by the U. S. Department of the Interior was soon passed. With an area over two square miles, this is the largest historic district in the United States.

Another major participant in the city's preservation has been the Savannah College of Art and Design. Since its beginning in 1979, SCAD has restored over forty buildings- mostly abandoned institutional buildings- in the Historic and Victorian Districts. They transformed the colonial era Habersham Street Jail into classrooms. SCAD students living near downtown have driven an ever growing demand for rental property. By the late nineties, interest spread far beyond the art school. Tourists, as well as locals, have rediscovered the charm of our enchanting city. After decades of decline, downtown is again the flourishing center of Savannah.

West Factor's Walk Prior to Restoration

photograph by Jeffrey Crowell

West Factor's Walk, Barnard Street Ramp

photograph courtesy of The Georgia Historical Society

West River Street, as seen from a photograph taken in 1936

photograph by Jeffrey Crowell

209-215 River Street

12   The corner of West Bryan and Jefferson Street, as it looked in the 30's

photograph by Jeffrey Crowell

West Bryan and Jefferson Street

photograph courtesy of The Georgia Historical Society

The 400 Block of West Bryan Street in 1927

The 4oo Block of West Bryan Street

photograph courtesy of The Georgia Historical Society

Established in 1790 in honor of Ben Franklin, Franklin Square was once known as the "Water Tank Square" to local residents. This photograph, taken in the year 1900, shows the water tower that was built in 1854.

photograph by Jeffrey Crowell

Franklin Square

18   This house, built in 1809, was moved from 219 West Jefferson to 425 East Bay Street

425 East Bay Street

photograph courtesy of The Georgia Historical Society

J. C. Penney Company circa 1937

photograph by Jeffrey Crowell

109 West Broughton Street

Vacant Lot on River Street

photograph by Jeffrey Crowell

West River Street

photograph courtesy of The Georgia Historical Society

M. Wilensky's General Store, 227 East Broughton

photograph by Jeffrey Crowell

Corner of East Broughton and Lincoln Street

Livingston Drugstore at 102 East Broughton

photograph by Jeffrey Crowell

Corner of East Broughton and Drayton Street

photograph courtesy of The Georgia Historical Society

Built in 1912 on the corner of Bull and Congress Street,
the Forest City Hotel Company Building housed Hotel Savannah.

photograph by Jeffrey Crowell

East Congress at Johnson Square

photograph courtesy of The Georgia Historical Society

Ocoma Garage at 21 Whitaker, the way it looked in the 1940's

photograph by Jeffrey Crowell

Parking Lot at 21 Whitaker Street

photograph courtesy of The Georgia Historical Society

Silver's 5 & 10 Store was once located at West Broughton and Barnard Street.

photograph by Jeffrey Crowell

201 West Broughton Street

An Ice Cream Store at 331 Whitaker as seen in 1935

photograph by Jeffrey Crowell

Parking Lot on Whitaker Street

This 1940 photograph shows the Odeon Theatre which was located at 136 East Broughton Street

photograph by Jeffrey Crowell

132 - 136 East Broughton Street

photograph courtesy of The Georgia Historical Society

In 1947, the Commercial Hotel was located at the corner of Barnard and Broughton Streets

photograph by Jeffrey Crowell

Corner of Barnard and Broughton Streets

In 1890, the Savannah Volunteer Guard purchased the property that had been the site of the Savannah Female Orphanage. The building pictured in this 1946 photograph was designed by Savannah Architect William G. Preston, who also designed the Cotton Exchange.

photograph by Jeffrey Crowell

340 Bull Street, the building was purchased and rennovated
by the Savannah College of Art and Design in its inaugural year of 1979.

Bull Street near 48th Street, as seen in this photograph taken in 1933

photograph by Jeffrey Crowell

Bull Street near 48th Street

The Blun Building at 35 Bull Street in this 1930 photograph

35 Bull Street

Bull Street looking north into Madison Square, with the DeSoto Hotel in th background

photograph by Jeffrey Crowell

Bull Street and Charlton Street

The corner of Bull Street and Henry Street in 1931

Bull Street at Herny Street

photograph courtesy of The Georgia Historical Society

Whitaker Street and Broughton Lane, as seen in 1933

photograph by Jeffrey Crowell

Whitaker Street and Broughton Lane

photograph courtesy of The Georgia Historical Society

Looking north on Drayton, toward the Cotton Exhange from a photograph taken in 1933

photograph by Jeffrey Crowell

Drayton Street at Congress Street

photograph courtesy of The Georgia Historical Society

Drayton at York Street as it looked in 1948

photograph by Jeffrey Crowell

Drayton at York Street

Built in 1905 on the site of the historic City Exchange, the City Hall building was designed by Savannah architect Hyman Witcover.

photograph courtesy of The Georgia Historical Society

photograph by Jeffrey Crowell

City Hall at Bay Street and Bull Street

The corner of Whitaker and Bay Street as seen in this 1930 photograph.

photograph courtesy of The Georgia Historical Society

photograph by Jeffrey Crowell

Whitaker at Bay Street

photograph courtesy of The Georgia Historical Society

In 1931, there was a DeSoto Car Dealership at 230 Drayton Street

Parking Lot at 230 Drayton Street

The corner of Abercorn and East York Street as seen in this 1962 photograph.

photograph by Jeffrey Crowell

The corner of Abercorn and East York Street on Oglethorpe Square

photograph courtesy of Steele Studio

Looking West on Broughton Street, circa 1922

Looking East on Broughton,
from Jefferson Street in 1946

photograph courtesy of The Georgia Historical Society

photograph courtesy of The Georgia Historical Society

East Broughton in the early 1900's

photograph by Jeffrey Crowell

East Broughton Street

photograph courtesy of The Georgia Historical Society

East Broughton, as seen in the 1920's

photograph by Jeffrey Crowell

East Broughton Street

photograph courtesy of The Georgia Historical Society

The Chatham Tire Company at 241 Drayton Street, as it appeared in 1938

photograph by Jeffrey Crowell

241 Drayton Street

photograph courtesy of The Georgia Historical Society

Built in 1797, the John D. Morgan House was moved from Warren Square to 24 Habersham Street

photograph by Jeffrey Crowell

24 Habersham Street

photograph courtesy of The Georgia Historical Society

The corner of East 37th Street and Lincoln in 1931

photograph by Jeffrey Crowell

East 37th Street and Lincoln Street

The Odd Fellows Building at 206 West State Street, as it appeared in 1935

photograph by Jeffrey Crowell

206 West State Street

Row houses in
the 400 block of
East Charlton Street

photograph courtesy of The Georgia Historical Society

The 400 block of East Charlton Street

West Bryan Street at the City Market in a 1934 photograph

photograph by Jeffrey Crowell

City Market Parking Garage

The house at 214 West Gwinnett was built in 1885. This was how it looked in 1938.

photograph by Jeffrey Crowell

Vacant Lot at 214 West Gwinnette Street

photograph courtesy of The Georgia Historical Society

15 East 36th Street from a photograph taken in 1934

photograph by Jeffrey Crowell

15 East 36th Street

photograph courtesy of The Georgia Historical Society

515 & 517 East Duffy Street in 1950

photograph by Jeffrey Crowell

515 & 517 East Duffy Street

City Market, Savannah, Ga.

photograph courtesy of Steele Studio

Ellis Square was laid out in 1733. The first City Market structure was built in 1763 and nearly destroyed by the great fire of 1796, which began in a bake shop. The second market burned in 1820 and was rebuilt two years later. That market was torn down and rebuilt in 1870 as seen in this photograph. In 1953, the market was demolished amid great controversy, which led to the formation of the Historic Savannah Foundation.

photograph courtesy of Steele Studio

The City Market at Ellis Square seen here in the early 1900's

photograph courtesy of The Georgia Historical Society

The City Market at St. Julian Street in 1934

St. Julian Street

The Cope House on West Hull Street in 1931

photograph by Jeffrey Crowell

Parking Lot on West Hull Street

St Mary's Orphanage was founded in 1875. The building shown in this 1931 photograph was built in 1883, and razed after the orphange moved to East Victory Drive in 1937.

photograph by Jeffrey Crowell

Apartments at 1604 Habersham Street

HOTEL GRAHAM
309 West Liberty St., Savannah, Ga.

photograph courtesy of Steele Studio

The Hotel Graham at 309 West Liberty Street

photograph by Jeffrey Crowell

Parking Lot at 309 West Liberty Street

The 1200 block of East 38th Street, as it looked in 1934.

The 1200 block of East 38th Street

photograph courtesy of The Georgia Historical Society

These Victorian houses on East Henry Street were built in 1881.

photograph by Jeffrey Crowell

220 - 228 East Henry Street

A 1920's view of the 200 block of East Duffy Street.

photograph by Jeffrey Crowell

East Duffy at Abercorn Street

photograph courtesy of The Georgia Historical Society

Harvey's Photography Studio on East Broughton Street

photograph by Jeffrey Crowell

14 - 17 East Broughton Street

A rare snowy day in Chippewa Square, circa 1914.

Chippewa Square

The grand Union Station was designed by Frank P. Milburn and officially opened for traffic in May of 1902.

The Main Waiting Room of the Union Station, circa 1955.

UNION DEPOT AND W BROAD STREET

photograph courtesy of The Georgia Historical Society

After sixty years of operation, the station closed in 1962 and was demolished the following year to make way for an Interstate 16 ramp.

photograph by Jeffrey Crowell

Interstate 16

The busy corner of West Broughton and Bull Street in the late forties.

West Broughton and Bull Street

Montgomery at 41st Street, as it looked in 1948.

photograph by Jeffrey Crowell

Montgomery at 41st Street

The General Offies of the the Savannah & Atlanta Railway

photograph by Jeffrey Crowell

Looking Over the new City Market

121

photograph courtesy of The Georgia Historical Society

Johnny Harris' Restaurant at 1651 Victory Drive as shown in this 1934 photograph.

photograph by Jeffrey Crowell

1651 Victory Drive

The Hotel Whitney,
at 9 Congress Street
in a 1940
photograph.

photograph courtesy of The Georgia Historical Society

photograph by Jeffrey Crowell

9 Congress Street

The Neal Blun Company
Commercial Buidling on
Bay Street in the 1920's

photograph courtesy of The Georgia Historical Society

photograph by Jeffrey Crowell

#2 West Bay Street

A view of the Savannah Harbor in the middle 1880's.

photograph by Jeffrey Crowell

The Savannah River and Talmadge Bridge

The residence at 324 Habersham prior to restoration.

photograph by Jeffrey Crowell

324 Habersham Street

132

This 1955 photograph shows a commercial block on West Broad Street,
now called Martin Luther King Jr. Blvd.

photograph by Jeffrey Crowell

Chatham County Jail

This house at 408 East Gaston, was built in 1892.

134

photograph courtesy of The Georgia Historical Society

photograph by Jeffrey Crowell

408 East Gaston Street

The 100 block of East Broughton as it looked in 1944.

photograph by Jeffrey Crowell

The 100 block of East Broughton Street

Citizens & Savings Building
from a 1945 photograph

photograph courtesy of The Georgia Historical Society

photograph by Jeffrey Crowell

Montgomery and Liberty Street

The Livingston Drugstore at 11 West Broughton as seen in this photograph from 1932.

West Broughton Street

Buildings in the 300 block of West Bryan Street

photograph by Jeffrey Crowell

The 300 block of West Bryan Street

Hotel Savannah in the 1940's

photograph courtesy of The Georgia Historical Society

32 Bull Street

photograph by Jeffrey Crowell

photograph courtesy of The Georgia Historical Society

Designed by William Jay and built in 1818, the Savannah Theatre was an opera and playhouse until 1931, when it began showing motion pictures. The original building burned in 1944 and again in 1948, was rebuilt and reopened in 1950. The photograph above was taken in 1905.

photograph by Jeffrey Crowell

The Savannah Theatre, at 222 Bull Street

photograph courtesy of The Georgia Historical Society

148 At #4 West Bryan, the Pulaski Hotel opened in 1850. It was one of Savannah's most popular hotels until being eclipsed by larger and grander hotels such as the DeSoto in the 1890's. This photograph was taken in 1933.

photograph by Jeffrey Crowell

The Corner of West Bryan and Bull Street

photograph courtesy of The Georgia Historical Society

Johnson Square, shown in this 1931 photograph, was Savannah's first square and was laid out in 1733.

Looking Over Johnson Square

photograph courtesy of Steele Studio

Castle Hall of the Knights of Pythias was located at the corner of York Street and Barnard Street.

photograph by Jeffrey Crowell

Federal Building

photograph courtesy of *The Georgia Historical Society*

The DeSoto Hotel opened on January 1, 1890, and remained Savannah's finest hotel until its close on January 1, 1965. Its six floors housed 206 rooms, solariums, various shops, and a restaurant.

The beautiful courtyard featured Japanese gardens and an outdoor pool. These photographs were taken in 1930.

photograph courtesy of *The Georgia Historical Society*

The DeSoto Hotel as seen in the 1920's

The DeSoto Hotel circa 1923

photograph by Jeffrey Crowell

The DeSoto Hilton Hotel

158　　Montgomery Cross Roads near Lake Mead in 1926.

photograph by Jeffrey Crowell

Montgomery Cross Roads

SAVANNAH, FROM
CITY EXCHANGE.

photograph courtesy of The Georgia Historical Society

Looking south on Bull Street in the 1930's

photograph courtesy of The Georgia Historical Society

162

photograph by Jeffrey Crowell

Looking south on Bull Street

Looking east down the Savannah River, as seen in this 1874 photograph.

164

photograph courtesy of The Georgia Historical Society

photograph by Jeffrey Crowell

Savannah's Riverfront

photograph courtesy of Steele Studio

St. Joseph Hospital was located at Taylor and Habersham Street between 1876 and 1900.

photograph by Jeffrey Crowell

Corner of Taylor and Habersham Street

photograph courtesy of Steele Studio

Estill Avenue was renamed Victory Drive as a memorial to the servicemen of World War I.

photograph by Jeffrey Crowell

Victory Drive at Atlantic Avenue

Chatham Artillery Armory,
Organized 1776,   Savannah, Ga.

photograph courtesy of Steele Studio

The Chatham Artillery Armory once stood on Wright Square, but was removed when
the Federal Building was enlarged in 1931.

photograph by Jeffrey Crowell

United States Federal Building

171